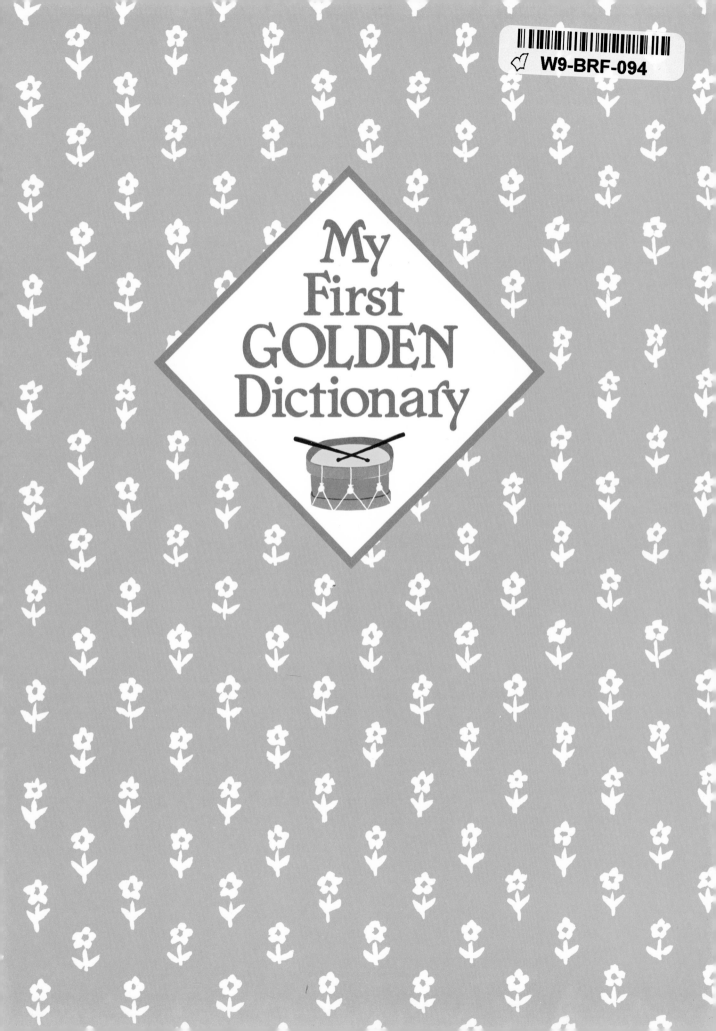

My
First
GOLDEN
Dictionary

My First GOLDEN Dictionary

By MARY REED
and EDITH OSSWALD

Illustrated by RICHARD SCARRY

A GOLDEN BOOK · NEW YORK

Western Publishing Company, Inc., Racine Wisconsin 53404

Using My First Golden Dictionary

MY FIRST GOLDEN DICTIONARY will be a treasure-book for every young child. Even the very youngest will enjoy the bright, familiar pictures. And for the beginning reader its hundreds of words represent familiar objects from everyday life. These words (chosen mainly from standard vocabulary lists of words familiar to children) are printed at the left of each column in large, clear type. Every word is pictured. And beneath each word is a short sentence—easy for the beginner to read—which repeats the object-word and tells something about it. The sentences appeal to the child's own interests. Thus word, picture, and sentence together help the child to read understandingly and to realize more keenly the connection between the printed word and his everyday world.

MY FIRST GOLDEN DICTIONARY can be used in many ways. The beginning reader will enjoy it by himself. A child just on the threshold of reading will enjoy the game of matching pictures with words he knows and also learning new words. And even the two-year-old will enjoy having the words and story-like sentences read to him as he looks at the bright, gay pictures.

Parents and teachers will think of many ways in which to make use of this book. But most important, we feel confident that no child will open MY FIRST GOLDEN DICTIONARY without enjoying it and wanting to explore the wonderful possibilities of the world of words. For bringing to children pleasure and delight in learning has been our primary aim.

MARY REED

A a

airplane
he **airplane** flies
gh up in the sky.

pple
he **apple** is good to eat,
risp and juicy and sweet.

pron
My **apron** keeps
y dress clean.

utomobile
We like to ride
n our **automobile.**

barn
A **barn** is a big house
for horses and cows.

basket
A **basket** is woven.
We carry things in it.

bathtub
The sailboat floats
in the **bathtub.**

beads
Beads are pretty.
I like to string them.

beans
Beans grow in pods.
We eat the **beans.**

B b

ball
The **ball** is round.
t will bounce.

balloon
The **balloon** is round.
t floats in the air.

banana
The **banana** is yellow.
I peel it and eat it.

bank
Pennies, nickels, and
dimes go into my **bank.**

bear
The **bear** sleeps all winter,
and wakes up in the spring.

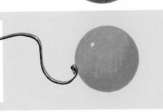

bed
Go to **bed,**
sleepyhead!

bee
Buzz, buzz, busy **bee!**
Fill your hive with honey.

beet
A **beet** is good to eat.
It grows in the ground.

bell
Ring the **bell** in school.
Ring the **bell** in church.

bicycle
My **bicycle** has a brake,
a bell, and two wheels.

bowl
My **bowl** holds soup.
Mother's **bowl** holds salad.

bird
Birds fly and sing.
They build nests, too.

box
What is in the **box**?
Let us open it and see.

birdhouse
The **birdhouse** hangs
from the branch of a tree.

boy
My brother is a **boy**.
My father was a **boy**.

blackboard
On my **blackboard**
I draw with chalk.

bread
I like **bread**.
It is good to eat.

blocks
Build a house of **blocks**.
Now build a wall.

bridge
The **bridge** crosses
the wide river.

bluebird
The **bluebird** sings
as he sits in the tree.
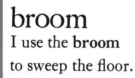

broom
I use the **broom**
to sweep the floor.

boat
My **boat** is small.
It will float on the water.

brush
This **brush** is for my hair.
That **brush** is for my clothes.

book
My **book** has
words and pictures.

bubbles
The soap **bubbles** I blow
soon float away and burst.

bookcase
This **bookcase** holds
my books in neat rows.

buffalo
The **buffalo** used to roam
the western plains.

bottle
See the **bottle** of milk.
Baby will drink it.

bug
A **bug** is small.
It may creep, fly, or crawl.

bus
The green **bus** carries children to school.

butterfly
The **butterfly** has colored wings.

button
Buttons are made for our clothes.

C c

camel
The **camel** carries a box across the desert.

can
A **can** is made of metal. It keeps food safe to eat.

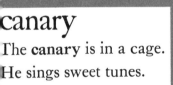

canary
The **canary** is in a cage. He sings sweet tunes.

candle
See the burning **candle** on my birthday cake.

candy
Candy is so sweet. It is very good to eat.

canoe
A **canoe** is a small boat. A paddle makes it go.

cards
We play with **cards**. We save picture **cards**.

carrot
The **carrot** is orange. Eat it cooked or raw.

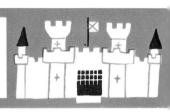

castle
A **castle** is home to a king and queen.

cat
The **cat** stretches out by the fire and purrs.

celery
Celery tastes good. It is a vegetable.

chain
The **chain** is strong. It is made of rings.

chair
This is my **chair**. I like to sit in it.

chalk
I write with **chalk** on the blackboard.

cherries
The **cherries** are red. I will pick some to eat.

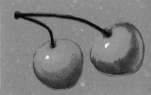

chest
I keep my clothes in a **chest** of drawers.

chicken
The baby **chicken** pecks and scratches.

corn
Corn grows very tall. I like to eat **corn**.

Christmas tree
Our **Christmas tree** is always pretty.

cow
The **cow** gives milk for her calf and me.

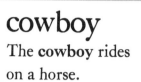

church
The **church** bells ring. People go to church.

cowboy
The **cowboy** rides on a horse.

clock
The **clock** always tells what time it is.

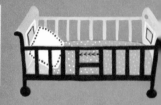

crayons
I use **crayons** to make my pictures bright.

clown
At the circus I like the funny **clown** best.

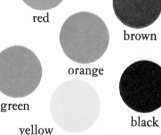

crib
The **crib** has high sides so Baby cannot fall out.

coat
My wool **coat** keeps me warm in winter.

colors
Red, orange, yellow, green, blue, purple, brown, and black are all **colors.**

red

brown

orange

green

yellow

black

purple

blue

D d

daisy
One **daisy** is white and one is yellow.

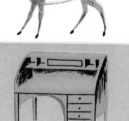

deer
The **deer** lives in the deep woods.

comb
I use a **comb** to keep my hair neat.

desk
I keep paper in my **desk.** I keep pencils there, too.

cooky
The **cooky** is sweet, and good to eat.

dime
My silver **dime** is worth ten copper pennies.

dishes

I put the **dishes** on the table for dinner.

dog

My **dog** is my friend. He likes to play.

doll

My **doll** can open and close both her eyes.

doll house

My **doll house** has tiny furniture in it.

donkey

A little **donkey** pulls a big wagon.

door

I open the **door** to go in. I can close it, too.

dress

Sister has a new **dress**. It has lace on the collar.

drum

Beat on the **drum**! Boom, boom, boom!

E e

Easter egg

I have an **Easter egg**. See the pretty colors.

elephant

The **elephant** has a trunk for a nose.

envelope

I put my letter in an **envelope**.

F f

farmer

A **farmer** raises plants and animals.

feather

Birds have **feathers** on their wings.

fire engine

The **fire engine** helps put out the fire.

fireman

A **fireman** fights a fire any time, day or night.

fish

I caught a **fish** with my fishing rod.

flag

Our country's **flag** flies over the school.

flashlight

I turn on my **flashlight**. It makes a beam of light.

flowers
In the spring, **flowers** grow in the garden.

fly
The **fly** is small and walks on the ceiling.

fork
I eat with a **fork**. It picks up food.

fox
The **fox** is clever. The **fox** is sly.

frog
At the pond the **frog** suns himself upon a log.

G g

gingerbread man
The **gingerbread man** is a tasty fellow.
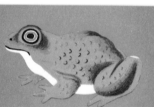

giraffe
A **giraffe** has a long neck and no voice.

girl
My mother was a **girl**. My sister is a **girl**.

glasses
My daddy wears **glasses** to help him see better.

goat
My **goat** has two horns. **Goats** give milk.

goldfish
The **goldfish** swims in a bowl all day.

goose
A baby **goose** is called a gosling.
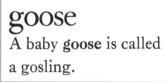

grapes
Purple **grapes** grow in bunches on a vine.

H h

handkerchief
My **handkerchief** has my name written on it.

hat
My **hat** fits my head, but the wind can blow it off.

haystack
The **haystack** keeps the hay dry for the cows.

heart
This red **heart** says, "Be my Valentine."

hen
The **hen** sits on her eggs until they hatch.

orn
you blow your **horn**
ou can make music.

orse
he **horse** can pull
heavy cart.

kitten
The **kitten** will grow up
to be a cat.

knife
The **knife** is sharp.
It cuts my meat.

I i

ce cream cone
like **ice cream cones**
ith chocolate ice cream.

nch
n **inch** is a small
nit of measure.

L l

lamp
The **lamp** has a bulb
which lights the room.

leaf
The **leaf** is flat and green.
It is part of a plant.

J j

lemon
With this **lemon**
we can make lemonade.

ack-o'-lantern
he **jack-o'-lantern** has
funny smile.

letter
I will send a **letter**
to my best friend.

Miss Sandra Halton
Holyoke, Mass

elly
elly and jam are good
o eat on a piece of bread.

Jelly

lettuce
I like **lettuce** leaves.
Rabbits like them, too.

lion
Listen to the **lion** roar!
He lives in the zoo.

K k

kite
My **kite** flies very high
when the wind blows.

lollipop
I like my **lollipop**.
It is sweet, hard, and good.

M m

man
My father is a **man**.
My brother will be one.

marbles
My **marbles** are round.
They are made of glass.

meat
We like to eat **meat**:
a steak or some chops.

merry-go-round
On the **merry-go-round**,
the horses run around.

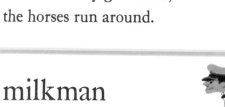

milkman
Milkman, bring us
milk and cream today.

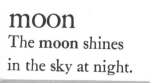

moon
The **moon** shines
in the sky at night.

mouse
The little **mouse** likes
crumbs and old cheese.

N n

needle
I thread the **needle**.
Then I sew.

nest
The birds make a **nest**.
The mother lays eggs in it.

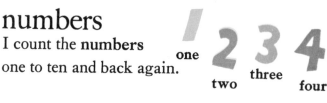

nickel
I have a **nickel**.
What shall I buy?

numbers
I count the **numbers**
one to ten and back again.

1 one
2 two
3 three
4 four
5 five
6 six
7 seven
8 eight
9 nine
10 ten

O o

orange
Oranges grow on a tree.
Oranges taste good.

overalls
Overalls are fun to wear.
I wear them every day.

owl
The **owl** hoots at night.
He hunts in the dark.

P p

paints
I use my **paints**
to make pretty pictures.

pajamas

My **pajamas** are striped.
I wear them every night.

pan

Mother cooks food
for supper in a **pan.**

pants

These are my long **pants.**
I feel grown-up now.

parrot

The **parrot** has feathers.
They are green and red.

peach

The **peach** is round
and juicy to eat.

peanut

Here is a **peanut.**
Roast it, crack it, eat it.

pear

This **pear** is yellow.
It is very juicy inside.

peas

Peas are round and green.
What a lot I can eat!

pen
My **pen** is full of ink.
It writes very well.

pencil
I write with my **pencil.**
It makes black lines.

penny

I have a shiny **penny.**
A penny is one cent.

piano

The **piano** has many keys.
They make pretty music.

pie

A **pie** has fruit inside.
It is baked in the oven.

pig

The **pig** lives in his pen.
He loves to eat and eat.

pineapple

A **pineapple** is prickly.
The inside is yellow.

pitcher

Here is a **pitcher** of tea.
Let us drink some now.

plum
Some **plums** are yellow,
but most are purple.

pocketbook
My **pocketbook** is full.
It has many things in it.

policeman

The **policeman** says "Go."
We can cross the street safely.

pony

I ride the little **pony.**
I sit on the saddle.

potato
I like baked **potatoes.**
I like them for supper.

ring
I have a new **ring.**
I wear it on my finger.

Q q

robin
Robin, chirp and sing!
You are a bird of spring.

quilt
A **quilt** is warm
to sleep under.

rooster
The **rooster** crows
when the sun comes up.

R r

rose
Roses smell sweet,
but watch out for thorns!

radio
Turn on the **radio**
to hear some music.

rubbers
Rubbers keep my feet
from getting wet.

radish
The red **radish** grows
in the ground.

S s

rainbow
I see a lovely **rainbow**
curving in the rainy sky.

sailboat
My **sailboat** can sail
when the wind blows.

raincoat
My **raincoat** has a cape.
It keeps me dry.

sandwich
A **sandwich** is something
good to eat at lunch.

record player
My **record player**
plays pretty music.

Santa Claus
Santa Claus brings us
toys at Christmas time.

reindeer
Santa has **reindeer**
to pull his sleigh.

scarecrow
The **scarecrow** scares
the crows away.

school

In **school** we learn how to read, write, and play.

scissors

I use the **scissors** to cut paper and string.

seal

The **seal** likes to swim and **catch** fish in the sea.

seashell

I found a **seashell** by the seashore.

seesaw

On the **seesaw**, up, down, and on the ground.

sheep
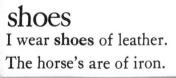
The **sheep** gives wool to wear, and food to eat.

ship
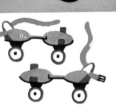
The big **ship** sails straight out to sea.

shoes

I wear **shoes** of leather. The horse's are of iron.

skates
Ice **skates** slide on the ice. Roller **skates** are also nice.

skirt
Sister has a new **skirt**. She wears it to school.

sled

I jump on my **sled**, and down the hill I go.

slippers

My **slippers** have bunnies on the toes.

snail
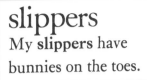
The **snail** creeps along with his house on his back.

snowman

We made a **snowman**. He melted in the sun.

snowsuit

My **snowsuit** is warm. It has a little brown hood.

socks

My feet fit in my **socks**. My **socks** fit in my shoes.

spider

The **spider** spins a web. He catches flies in it.

spoon

My **spoon** is silver. I use it to eat my soup.

squirrel
The **squirrel** in the tree, takes a nut from me.

star

Little **star**, far away, I see you twinkling at night.

steamshovel
My little **steamshovel**
digs in the sand box.

stove
Mother's **stove** gets hot.
The heat cooks our food.

strawberry
The **strawberry** is red.
It is very good to eat.

suit
My new **suit** is blue.
My daddy's **suit** is new.

suitcase
In my **suitcase** I put
my clothes when I travel.

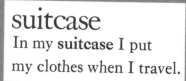

sun
The **sun** shines brightly.
It makes us warm.

swan
The **swan** is swimming.
He is a beautiful bird.

sweater
My **sweater** is soft.
It is made from wool.

T t

table
Our **table** has four legs.
We eat at the **table**.

taxi
The **taxi** meter ticks and
shows us what to pay.

Teddy bear
Teddy bear is my toy.
He is round and furry.

telephone
I talk on the **telephone**.
I can talk to my friends.

television
The funniest shows are
on the **television** screen.

tent
The **tent** is high on top
and low on the sides.

tiger
The **tiger** does not like
to live in a cage.

tomato
I pick **tomatoes** to eat
when they are ripe.

toothbrush
Use a **toothbrush** on
your teeth every day.

top
Pull the string, spin the **top**.
See it spin, see it stop.

tractor
A **tractor** pulls a plow,
and does farm work.

train
The **train** goes down the track.

tree
A big **tree** gives shade on hot summer days.

tricycle
My **tricycle** goes fast on three wheels.

truck
On the highway **trucks** carry loads to the city.

tugboat
The **tugboat** is very strong. It moves big ships along.

turkey
The **turkey** is proud. He spreads his big tail.

turtle
The **turtle** wears a shell. It protects him well.

U u

umbrella
My **umbrella** keeps me dry in bad weather.

underwear
The **underwear** hangs on the line to dry.

V v

valentine
This **valentine** says, "I like you, Mary."

vase
The **vase** holds mother's pretty bunch of flowers.

violet
Purple **violets** grow on long green stalks.

violin
The **violin** sings when I play the strings.

W w

watch
Daddy's **watch** goes "tick tock, tick tock."

watermelon
Green **watermelon**, I will eat a slice of you.

whale
The huge **whale** lives in the ocean.

wheelbarrow
I push my **wheelbarrow**. I fill it with toys.

window

My **window** is open.
The wind blows in.

witch

A **witch** rides a broom,
but never is seen.

wolf
The **wolf** is wild.
He hunts by night.

woman

My mother is a **woman**.
My sister will be one.

Y y

yarn

Knit the **yarn** to make
sweaters and socks.

Z z

zipper
Zip! A **zipper** goes
up or down very fast.

zoo
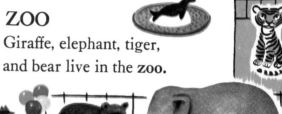
Giraffe, elephant, tiger,
and bear live in the **zoo**.

X x

xylophone

Strike a tune
on the **xylophone**.

1 2 3 4 5 6 7
8 9 10 11 12

Aa Bb Cc Dd Ee
Ff Gg Hh Ii Jj
Kk Ll Mm Nn Oo
Pp Qq Rr Ss Tt
Uu Vv Ww
Xx Yy Zz